Fractions & Decimals (Advanced)

3rd Grade Math Workbook Series

BABY PROFESSOR

EDUCATION KIDS

Compare 2 proper fractions
(with pie charts)

Compare the fractions,
and write > or < or = between them.

1. 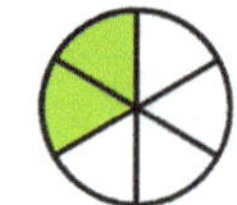

$$\frac{2}{6} \qquad \frac{5}{8}$$

5. 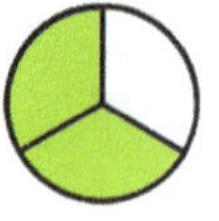

$$\frac{2}{3} \qquad \frac{4}{8}$$

2.  

$$\frac{4}{8} \qquad \frac{2}{7}$$

6. 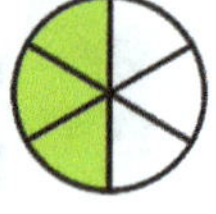

$$\frac{3}{6} \qquad \frac{1}{4}$$

3.  

$$\frac{1}{3} \qquad \frac{4}{8}$$

7. 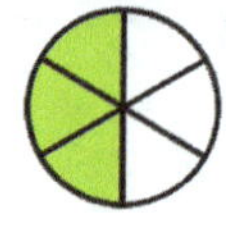 

$$\frac{3}{6} \qquad \frac{4}{8}$$

4. 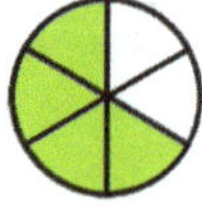

$$\frac{4}{6} \qquad \frac{5}{8}$$

8. 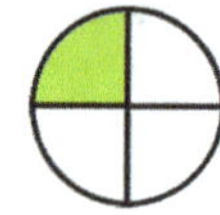 

$$\frac{1}{4} \qquad \frac{2}{6}$$

9. 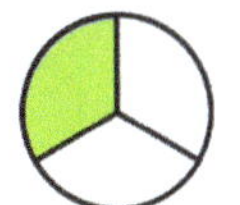 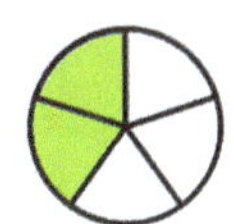

$\dfrac{1}{3}$ $\qquad$ $\dfrac{2}{5}$

10. 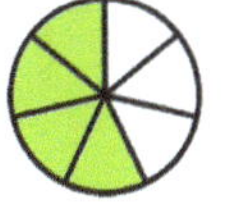 

$\dfrac{4}{7}$ $\qquad$ $\dfrac{1}{5}$

11. 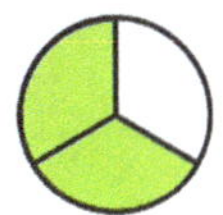

$\dfrac{4}{8}$ $\qquad$ $\dfrac{2}{3}$

12. 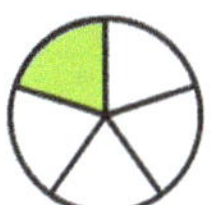

$\dfrac{3}{7}$ $\qquad$ $\dfrac{1}{5}$

13. 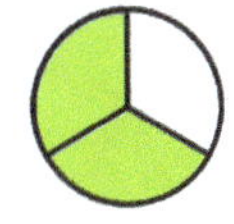

$\dfrac{2}{3}$ $\qquad$ $\dfrac{3}{8}$

14. 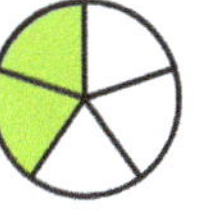 

$\dfrac{2}{5}$ $\qquad$ $\dfrac{4}{8}$

15. 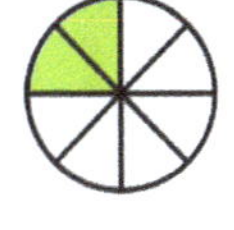 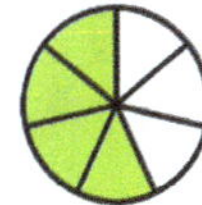

$\dfrac{2}{8}$ $\qquad$ $\dfrac{4}{7}$

16. 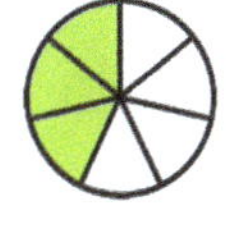 

$\dfrac{3}{7}$ $\qquad$ $\dfrac{4}{5}$

17. 

$$\frac{2}{3} \qquad \frac{4}{5}$$

21. 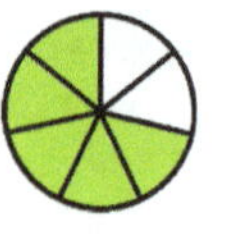

$$\frac{5}{7} \qquad \frac{2}{6}$$

18. 

$$\frac{7}{8} \qquad \frac{3}{4}$$

22. 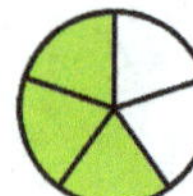

$$\frac{2}{8} \qquad \frac{3}{5}$$

19. 

$$\frac{4}{7} \qquad \frac{6}{8}$$

23.

$$\frac{2}{5} \qquad \frac{6}{7}$$

20. 

$$\frac{1}{3} \qquad \frac{3}{7}$$

24.

$$\frac{2}{4} \qquad \frac{1}{3}$$

25.

$$\frac{3}{7} \qquad \frac{5}{8}$$

26.

$$\frac{4}{8} \qquad \frac{3}{4}$$

27.

$$\frac{2}{6} \qquad \frac{5}{7}$$

28.

$$\frac{5}{6} \qquad \frac{6}{7}$$

29. 

$$\frac{3}{8} \qquad \frac{6}{7}$$

30. 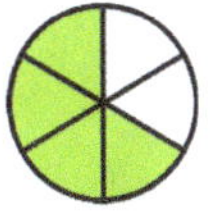

$$\frac{4}{6} \qquad \frac{3}{5}$$

31. 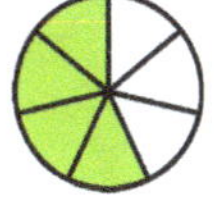

$$\frac{4}{7} \qquad \frac{1}{4}$$

32. 

$$\frac{5}{8} \qquad \frac{3}{7}$$

33. 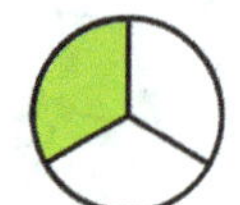 $\dfrac{2}{5}$ $\dfrac{1}{3}$

34.  $\dfrac{3}{7}$ $\dfrac{1}{4}$

35.  $\dfrac{4}{6}$ $\dfrac{1}{3}$

36.  $\dfrac{5}{7}$ $\dfrac{4}{8}$

37.  $\dfrac{7}{8}$ $\dfrac{4}{7}$

38.  $\dfrac{4}{8}$ $\dfrac{1}{6}$

39.  $\dfrac{1}{5}$ $\dfrac{4}{8}$

40. 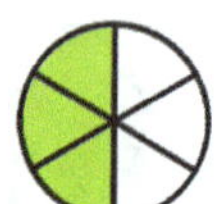 $\dfrac{5}{8}$ $\dfrac{3}{6}$

41. 

$$\frac{3}{6} \qquad \frac{6}{7}$$

42. 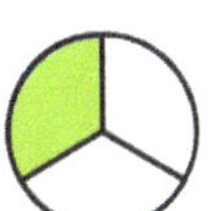

$$\frac{3}{4} \qquad \frac{1}{3}$$

43. 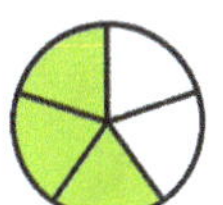

$$\frac{5}{8} \qquad \frac{3}{5}$$

44. 

$$\frac{4}{6} \qquad \frac{3}{4}$$

45. 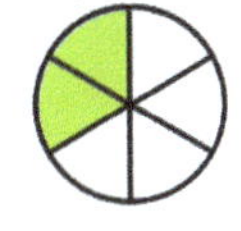

$$\frac{2}{6} \qquad \frac{4}{5}$$

46. 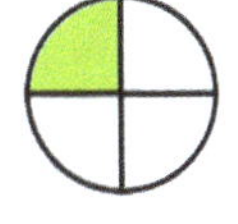

$$\frac{1}{4} \qquad \frac{2}{8}$$

47. 

$$\frac{3}{5} \qquad \frac{6}{8}$$

48. 

$$\frac{7}{8} \qquad \frac{4}{7}$$

49. 

$\dfrac{5}{7}$ $\dfrac{4}{5}$

53. 

$\dfrac{2}{6}$ $\dfrac{1}{5}$

50.

$\dfrac{5}{6}$ $\dfrac{2}{4}$

54. 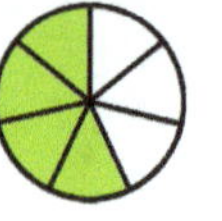

$\dfrac{4}{7}$ $\dfrac{2}{8}$

51.

$\dfrac{4}{7}$ $\dfrac{7}{8}$

55. 

$\dfrac{6}{8}$ $\dfrac{4}{6}$

52.

$\dfrac{3}{6}$ $\dfrac{1}{4}$

56. 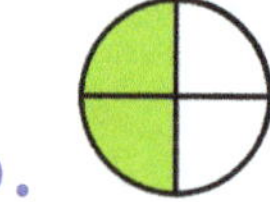

$\dfrac{2}{4}$ $\dfrac{5}{6}$

57. 

$$\frac{3}{6} \qquad \frac{6}{7}$$

59.  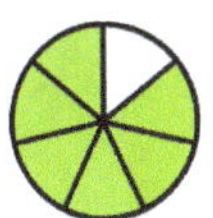

$$\frac{4}{8} \qquad \frac{6}{7}$$

58. 

$$\frac{3}{8} \qquad \frac{1}{7}$$

60. 

$$\frac{2}{4} \qquad \frac{1}{7}$$

Compare 2 proper or improper fractions (with pie charts)

Compare the fractions,
and write > or < or = between them.

1. 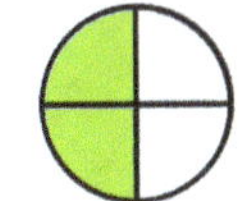 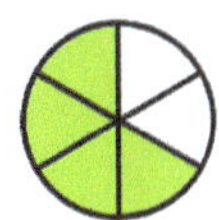

$$\frac{2}{4} \qquad \frac{4}{6}$$

5. 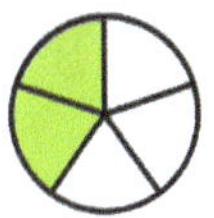

$$\frac{2}{5} \qquad \frac{3}{8}$$

2. 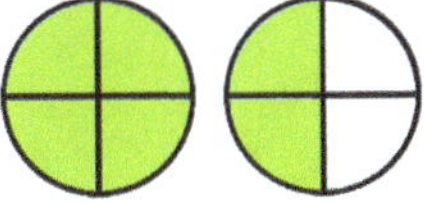

$$\frac{6}{4} \qquad \frac{8}{5}$$

6. 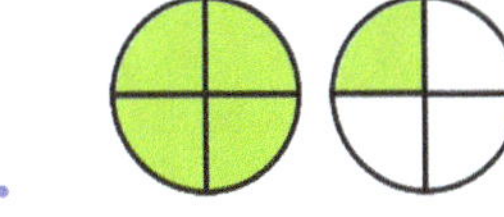 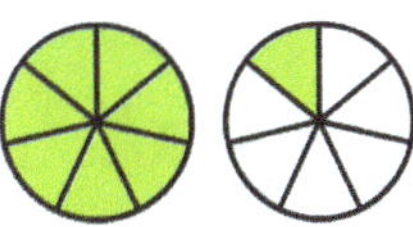

$$\frac{5}{4} \qquad \frac{8}{7}$$

3. 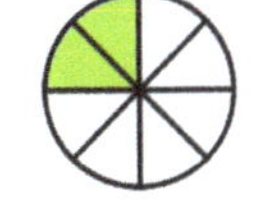 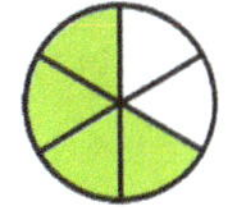

$$\frac{2}{8} \qquad \frac{4}{6}$$

7. 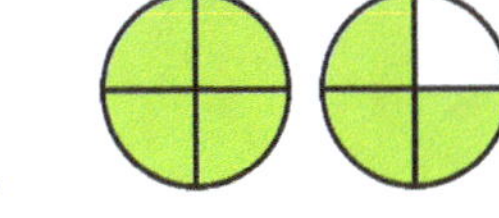 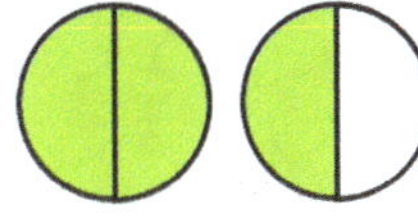

$$\frac{7}{4} \qquad \frac{3}{2}$$

4. 

$$\frac{4}{7} \qquad \frac{1}{6}$$

8. 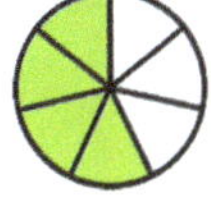  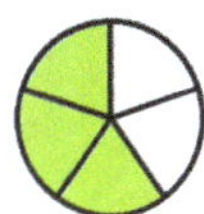

$$\frac{5}{7} \qquad \frac{3}{5}$$

9. 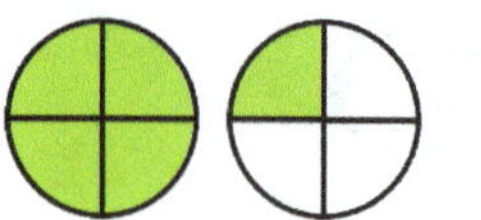

$$\frac{5}{4}$$

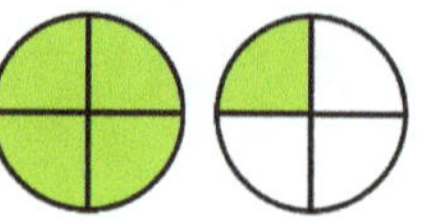

$$\frac{6}{7}$$

13. 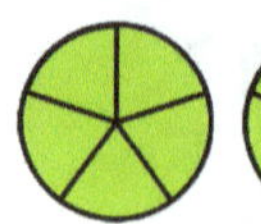

$$\frac{5}{4}$$

$$\frac{7}{5}$$

10. 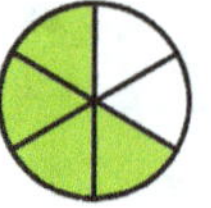

$$\frac{4}{7}$$

$$\frac{2}{6}$$

14. 

$$\frac{3}{7}$$

$$\frac{4}{6}$$

11.

$$\frac{1}{5}$$

$$\frac{4}{6}$$

15.

$$\frac{3}{5}$$

$$\frac{4}{8}$$

12. 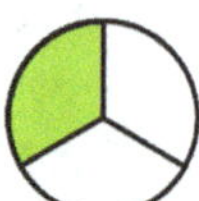

$$\frac{5}{6}$$

$$\frac{1}{3}$$

16. 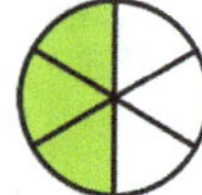

$$\frac{6}{7}$$

$$\frac{3}{6}$$

17.
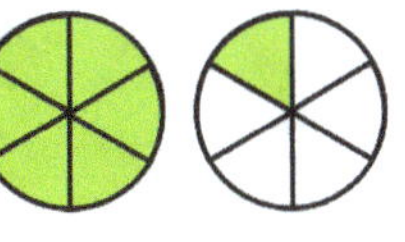

$$\frac{5}{7}$$

$$\frac{6}{5}$$

20.
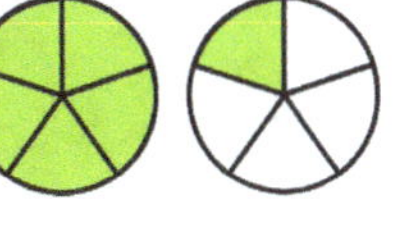

$$\frac{7}{6}$$

$$\frac{4}{5}$$

18.
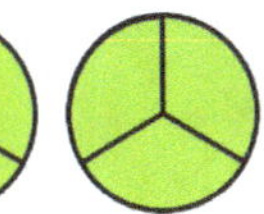
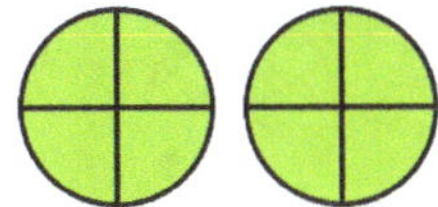

$$\frac{5}{7}$$

$$\frac{3}{5}$$

21.
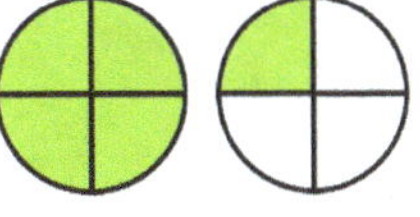

$$\frac{5}{4}$$

$$\frac{7}{8}$$

19.
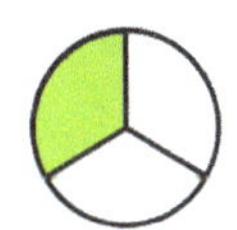

$$\frac{7}{3}$$

$$\frac{8}{4}$$

22.
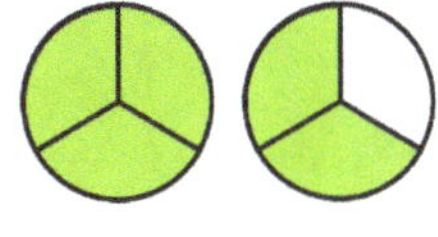

$$\frac{6}{5}$$

$$\frac{5}{7}$$

23.
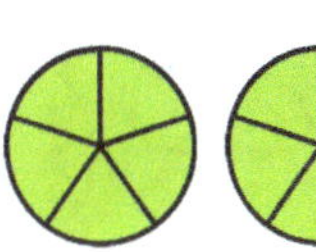

$$\frac{5}{3}$$

$$\frac{8}{5}$$

24. 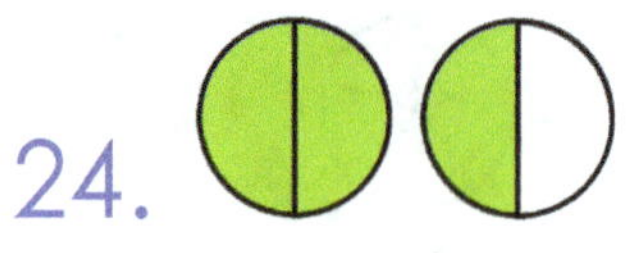

$$\frac{3}{2}$$

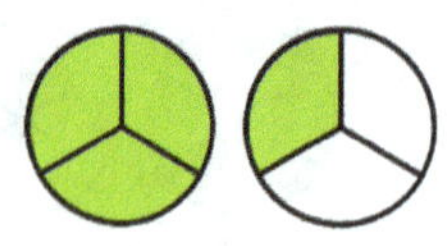

$$\frac{4}{3}$$

28. 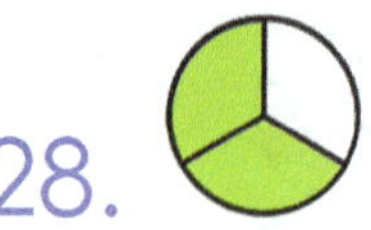

$$\frac{2}{3}$$

$$\frac{6}{7}$$

25. 

$$\frac{4}{7}$$

$$\frac{3}{5}$$

29.

$$\frac{2}{5}$$

$$\frac{1}{6}$$

26.

$$\frac{4}{3}$$

$$\frac{7}{6}$$

30. 

$$\frac{2}{6}$$

$$\frac{1}{8}$$

27.

$$\frac{7}{4}$$

$$\frac{2}{1}$$

31. 

$$\frac{3}{5}$$

$$\frac{1}{8}$$

32. 

$$\frac{5}{6}$$ $$\frac{8}{7}$$

35. 

$$\frac{2}{8}$$ $$\frac{4}{7}$$

33. 

$$\frac{2}{3}$$ $$\frac{5}{6}$$

36. 

$$\frac{7}{8}$$ $$\frac{2}{5}$$

34. 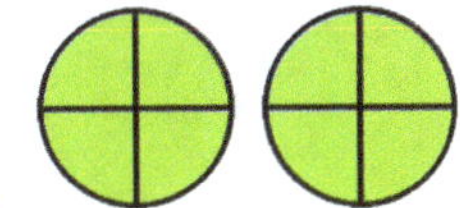

$$\frac{8}{4}$$ $$\frac{5}{2}$$

37.  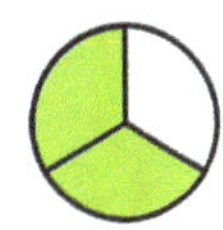

$$\frac{6}{8}$$ $$\frac{2}{3}$$

38. 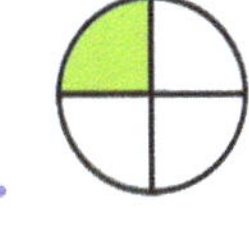 

$$\frac{1}{4}$$ $$\frac{2}{8}$$

39. 

$$\frac{3}{5} \qquad \frac{7}{8}$$

43. 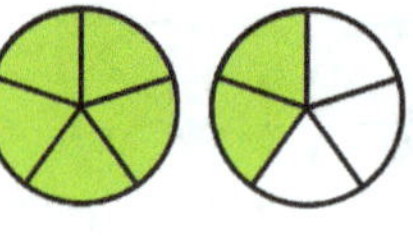 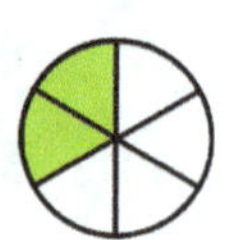

$$\frac{7}{5} \qquad \frac{8}{6}$$

40. 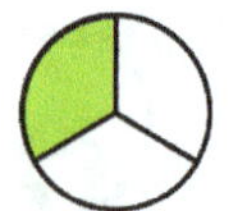 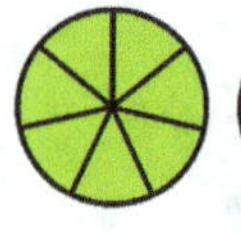

$$\frac{8}{7} \qquad \frac{7}{8}$$

44. 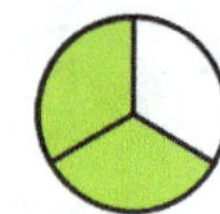

$$\frac{5}{8} \qquad \frac{2}{3}$$

41. 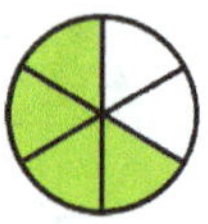

$$\frac{4}{7} \qquad \frac{1}{3}$$

45. 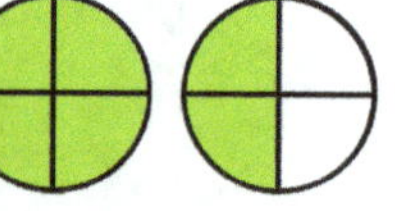

$$\frac{6}{4} \qquad \frac{8}{7}$$

42. 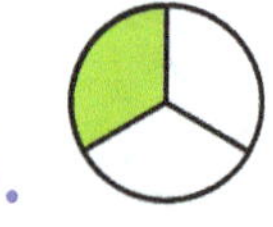

$$\frac{2}{4} \qquad \frac{4}{6}$$

46. 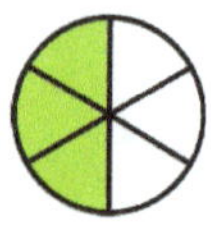

$$\frac{1}{3} \qquad \frac{3}{6}$$

47. 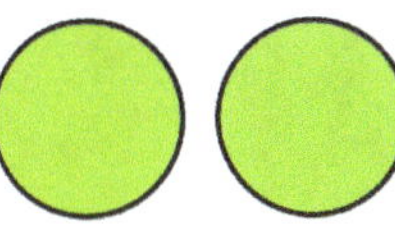 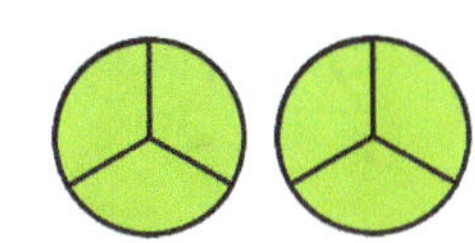

$$\frac{2}{1}$$

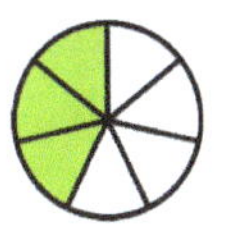 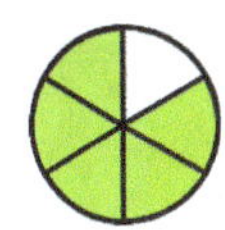

$$\frac{7}{3}$$

50.  

$$\frac{3}{7} \qquad \frac{5}{6}$$

48. 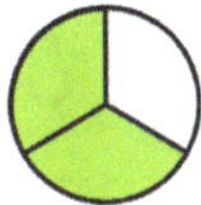

$$\frac{4}{8} \qquad \frac{2}{3}$$

51.

$$\frac{5}{6} \qquad \frac{3}{8}$$

49. 

$$\frac{1}{3} \qquad \frac{2}{8}$$

52.  

$$\frac{1}{5} \qquad \frac{2}{7}$$

53. 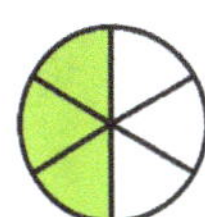

$$\frac{1}{8} \qquad \frac{3}{6}$$

54. 

$$\frac{2}{8}$$ $$\frac{1}{7}$$

55. 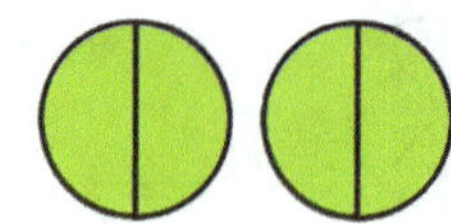 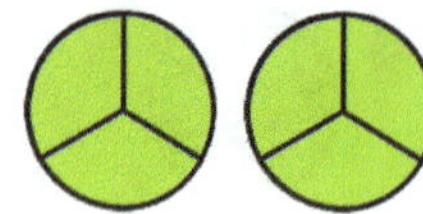

$$\frac{5}{2}$$ $$\frac{7}{3}$$

56. 

$$\frac{3}{4}$$ $$\frac{4}{8}$$

57. 

$$\frac{3}{4}$$ $$\frac{6}{7}$$

58.  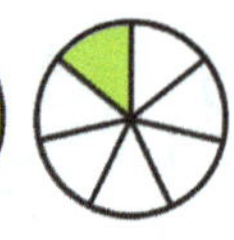

$$\frac{7}{8}$$ $$\frac{6}{7}$$

59.  

$$\frac{7}{8}$$ $$\frac{8}{7}$$

60.

$$\frac{1}{8}$$ $$\frac{2}{6}$$

Adding like fractions - denominators from 2-12

1. $\dfrac{7}{5} + \dfrac{3}{5} =$

2. $\dfrac{8}{7} + \dfrac{8}{7} =$

3. $\dfrac{1}{6} + \dfrac{12}{6} =$

4. $\dfrac{2}{7} + \dfrac{10}{7} =$

5. $\dfrac{12}{8} + \dfrac{1}{8} =$

6. $\dfrac{7}{12} + \dfrac{3}{12} =$

7. $\dfrac{8}{12} + \dfrac{6}{12} =$

8. $\dfrac{8}{9} + \dfrac{1}{9} =$

9. $\dfrac{5}{12} + \dfrac{10}{12} =$

10. $\dfrac{7}{3} + \dfrac{5}{3} =$

11. $\dfrac{8}{6} + \dfrac{3}{6} =$

12. $\dfrac{2}{5} + \dfrac{4}{5} =$

13. $\dfrac{11}{12} + \dfrac{10}{12} =$

14. $\dfrac{11}{10} + \dfrac{6}{10} =$

15. $\dfrac{7}{3} + \dfrac{1}{3} =$

16. $\dfrac{10}{3} + \dfrac{4}{3} =$

17. $\dfrac{7}{6} + \dfrac{1}{6} =$

18. $\dfrac{1}{2} + \dfrac{11}{2} =$

19. $\dfrac{10}{3} + \dfrac{10}{3} =$

20. $\dfrac{8}{6} + \dfrac{1}{6} =$

21. $\dfrac{10}{9} + \dfrac{2}{9} =$

22. $\dfrac{1}{5} + \dfrac{1}{5} =$

23. $\dfrac{2}{6} + \dfrac{7}{6} =$

24. $\dfrac{5}{7} + \dfrac{1}{7} =$

25. $\dfrac{4}{10} + \dfrac{6}{10} =$

26. $\dfrac{3}{10} + \dfrac{9}{10} =$

27. $\dfrac{10}{3} + \dfrac{11}{3} =$

28. $\dfrac{5}{10} + \dfrac{4}{10} =$

29. $\dfrac{7}{10} + \dfrac{8}{10} =$

30. $\dfrac{7}{5} + \dfrac{1}{5} =$

Subtracting like fractions (denominators 2-12)

1. $\dfrac{10}{3} - \dfrac{4}{3} =$

2. $\dfrac{4}{5} - \dfrac{1}{5} =$

3. $\dfrac{5}{11} - \dfrac{5}{11} =$

4. $\dfrac{12}{10} - \dfrac{2}{10} =$

5. $\dfrac{12}{10} - \dfrac{11}{10} =$

6. $\dfrac{4}{8} - \dfrac{1}{8} =$

7. $\dfrac{5}{8} - \dfrac{2}{8} =$

8. $\dfrac{6}{10} - \dfrac{5}{10} =$

9. $\dfrac{11}{4} - \dfrac{11}{4} =$

10. $\dfrac{8}{7} - \dfrac{4}{7} =$

11. $\dfrac{7}{2} - \dfrac{5}{2} =$

12. $\dfrac{9}{4} - \dfrac{1}{4} =$

13. $\dfrac{9}{6} - \dfrac{5}{6} =$

14. $\dfrac{3}{6} - \dfrac{2}{6} =$

15. $\dfrac{12}{3} - \dfrac{11}{3} =$ 23. $\dfrac{10}{7} - \dfrac{8}{7} =$

16. $\dfrac{11}{9} - \dfrac{7}{9} =$ 24. $\dfrac{8}{7} - \dfrac{4}{7} =$

17. $\dfrac{11}{6} - \dfrac{4}{6} =$ 25. $\dfrac{11}{4} - \dfrac{7}{4} =$

18. $\dfrac{8}{12} - \dfrac{8}{12} =$ 26. $\dfrac{12}{11} - \dfrac{12}{11} =$

19. $\dfrac{11}{10} - \dfrac{3}{10} =$ 27. $\dfrac{7}{2} - \dfrac{5}{2} =$

20. $\dfrac{12}{8} - \dfrac{3}{8} =$ 28. $\dfrac{9}{12} - \dfrac{7}{12} =$

21. $\dfrac{7}{11} - \dfrac{4}{11} =$ 29. $\dfrac{9}{3} - \dfrac{1}{3} =$

22. $\dfrac{1}{9} - \dfrac{1}{9} =$ 30. $\dfrac{12}{6} - \dfrac{3}{6} =$

Decimal Addition

Solve.

1. 1.7 + 0.2 = _____

2. 0.0 + 1.1 = _____

3. 0.7 + 0.3 = _____

4. 1.4 + 1.1 = _____

5. 2.8 + 1.1 = _____

6. 0.4 + 1.8 = _____

7. 0.9 + 0.5 = _____

8. 0.8 + 1.7 = _____

9. 1.6 + 0.6 = _____

10. 0.9 + 1.6 = _____

11. 2.0 + 1.6 = _____

12. 1.7 + 1.0 = _____

13. 0.0 + 0.3 = _____

14. 0.6 + 0.4 = _____

15. 1.9 + 1.7 = _____

16. 0.9 + 1.7 = _____

17. 1.1 + 0.7 = _____

18. 0.2 + 0.7 = _____

19. 2.6 + 1.5 = _____

20. 0.1 + 1.7 = _____

Decimal Subtraction

Solve.

1. 3.5 − 2.3 = _______
2. 3.3 − 2.1 = _______
3. 4.1 − 0.5 = _______
4. 5.7 − 0.8 = _______
5. 6.0 − 1.6 = _______
6. 5.8 − 0.9 = _______
7. 2.7 − 1.7 = _______
8. 10.3 − 2.7 = _______
9. 5.1 − 4.4 = _______
10. 7.0 − 3.8 = _______
11. 5.6 − 5.4 = _______
12. 5.6 − 0.9 = _______
13. 4.3 − 3.7 = _______
14. 5.5 − 4.1 = _______
15. 4.8 − 3.9 = _______
16. 1.9 − 0.2 = _______
17. 5.7 − 0.6 = _______
18. 7.5 − 5.5 = _______
19. 4.0 − 2.4 = _______
20. 4.6 − 2.0 = _______

Compare 2 proper fractions (with pie charts)

1.	<	16.	<	31.	>	46.	=
2.	>	17.	<	32.	>	47.	<
3.	<	18.	>	33.	>	48.	>
4.	>	19.	<	34.	>	49.	<
5.	>	20.	<	35.	>	50.	>
6.	>	21.	>	36.	>	51.	<
7.	=	22.	<	37.	>	52.	>
8.	<	23.	<	38.	>	53.	>
9.	<	24.	>	39.	<	54.	>
10.	>	25.	<	40.	>	55.	>
11.	<	26.	<	41.	<	56.	<
12.	>	27.	<	42.	>	57.	<
13.	>	28.	<	43.	>	58.	>
14.	<	29.	<	44.	<	59.	<
15.	<	30.	>	45.	<	60.	>

Compare 2 proper or improper fractions (with pie charts)

1. <	16. >	31. >	46. <
2. <	17. <	32. <	47. <
3. <	18. >	33. <	48. <
4. >	19. >	34. <	49. >
5. >	20. >	35. <	50. <
6. >	21. >	36. >	51. >
7. >	22. >	37. >	52. <
8. >	23. >	38. =	53. <
9. >	24. >	39. <	54. >
10. >	25. <	40. >	55. >
11. <	26. >	41. >	56. >
12. >	27. <	42. <	57. <
13. <	28. <	43. >	58. >
14. <	29. >	44. <	59. <
15. >	30. >	45. >	60. <

Adding like fractions - denominators from 2-12

1.	2	16.	4
2.	2 2	17.	4
3.	7	18.	1 5
4.	2 1	19.	6
5.	6	20.	1 1
6.	1 5	21.	5
7.	7	22.	1 3
8.	1 5	23.	4
9.	8	24.	1 7
10.	5	25.	10
11.	6	26.	2 2
12.	1 1	27.	3
13.	6	28.	4 2
14.	1	29.	3
15.	1 1	30.	1 1

Subtracting like fractions (denominators 2-12)

1. 2	16. 7
2. 3	17. 1
3. 5	18. 2
4. 0	19. 2
5. 1	20. 3
6. 1	21. 1
7. 10	22. 6
8. 3	23. 1
9. 8	24. 3
10. 3	25. 4
11. 8	26. 9
12. 1	27. 11
13. 10	28. 6
14. 0	29. 0
15. 4	30. 4

Decimal Addition

1. 1.9
2. 1.1
3. 1
4. 2.5
5. 3.9

6. 2.2
7. 1.4
8. 2.5
9. 2.2
10. 2.5

11. 3.6
12. 2.7
13. 0.3
14. 1
15. 3.6

16. 2.6
17. 1.8
18. 0.9
19. 4.1
20. 1.8

Decimal Subtraction

1. 1.2
2. 1.2
3. 3.6
4. 4.9
5. 4.4

6. 4.9
7. 1
8. 7.6
9. 0.7
10. 3.2

11. 0.2
12. 4.7
13. 0.6
14. 1.4
15. 0.9

16. 1.7
17. 5.1
18. 2
19. 1.6
20. 2.6

www.ingramcontent.com/pod-product-compliance
Lightning Source LLC
Chambersburg PA
CBHW080821120726
48001CB00009B/2958